Hugo Mulertt

How to Cook Fish

Recipes for Preparing Sea and Fresh Water Fish for the Table

Hugo Mulertt

How to Cook Fish
Recipes for Preparing Sea and Fresh Water Fish for the Table

ISBN/EAN: 9783744794855

Printed in Europe, USA, Canada, Australia, Japan

Cover: Foto ©Lupo / pixelio.de

More available books at **www.hansebooks.com**

HOW TO COOK FISH.

Vereini

HOW TO COOK FISH.

RECIPES

FOR PREPARING

SEA AND FRESH WATER FISH FOR THE TABLE.

COLLECTED BY THE

VEREIN DEUTSCHER FISCH HAENDLER

(Society of German Fish-Dealers, Germany).

FROM THE GERMAN, WITH ADDITIONS, BY

HUGO MULERTT,

A. C. Imp. Russian Soc. of Acclimation. Author of "The Goldfish and its Culture."

CINCINNATI, OHIO.
1886.

PREFACE

FISH, as food, are by the great majority of the people underestimated. Now this is wrong! Fish constitute, according to the highest authorities of the present time, not only a wholesome and nourishing food for man, but fish-diet is even declared *necessary* for the welfare of the human body. According to recent researches made under the auspices of the Smithsonian Institution, a pound of Herring, Salmon or Whitefish is equal, in nourishing qualities, to a pound of the best fresh beef. In the presence of this fact, fish can not be looked upon as a luxury, and fish-culture has as important a mission to fulfill as cattle-raising.

When, in former ages, the learned monks set apart one day of each week for fish-diet, they, no doubt, understood the influence of fish-diet on the human system. It is, furthermore, a historical fact, that most epidemics that raged in Central Europe prevailed in those days when fish-culture was in a very neglected condition.

But even if all this were left out of consideration, fish is such excellent eating, constitutes such an agreeable change in the daily bill of fare, that the author hopes this little work will meet with the approval of every housewife.

INTRODUCTION.

———

BEFORE we treat of the different manners and styles of cooking fish, it is necessary that we become somewhat posted about fish in general. Do not be afraid however, for I shall not tire you with a lecture on the natural history of fish; I shall merely state what is

NECESSARY FOR YOU

to know in regard to dead fish, as we have nothing, at least very little, to do with the living fish in this work.

In Holland, where the people know more about the cooking of a fish than in any other country of the world—where fish-cooking is considered almost a science—fish are killed as soon as caught, or, anyway, as soon as practicable thereafter.

Any person who has had the opportunity

TO EAT FISH

in that country, either in a public restaurant or

at a family table, will have noticed the much finer flavor and the firmness of its flesh. These qualities are, for the greater part, due to the manner in which the fish are killed. Let us see on what this is based. Fish breathe through gills which are located in the head; the water taken in at the mouth is forced through them, and thus the fine bloodvessels that are contained in these gills are enabled to absorb the oxygen contained in the water for the blood of the fish. As soon as

A FISH IS TAKEN

from its element, the water, these gills are unable to supply the blood any longer with the necessary oxygen, and the consequence is, a horrible death-struggle of shorter or longer duration, according to the variety of fish, which ends in a painful death by suffocation.

But not alone will fish die of suffocation out of their element, they will also die of the same cause if too large a number are kept in an insufficient quality and quantity of water.

It would be deemed ridiculous to expect any person to eat of the meat of cattle or poultry that came to its death by suffocation. And so it is. Meat of animals, whether poultry or fish, that have died of disease, is unwholesome as food for man.

Right here we may have the explanation for the dislike some people manifest against fish-diet, "because it lies so heavy in their stomachs;" for this dislike may have had its origin in the condition of the fish-meat, rather than in the incorrect manner by which it was prepared for the table.

The proper and least cruel way

TO KILL A FISH

is—the quickest way. Take a small, pointed, sharp knife, insert it immediately behind the fish's head and cut the spinal column. The meat of a fish thus killed is wholesome, and will keep in a good condition for several days, if kept in a well-ventilated, cool place; while that of a fish which was slowly smothered to death, either in or out of water, will rapidly decay, on account of the absence of a sufficient quantity of oxygen in its blood.

A DEAD FISH

should never come in contact with water until just before it is to be cooked, as water takes the fine flavor from it, and also a great part of its nourishing qualities. When a fish is killed in the manner described above, scale it, cut it into pieces if necessary, and then wipe it dry with a towel. In this condition, place it in a cool, well-ventilated place. If

this should be your ice-box, do not lay it directly on
the ice ; if it be the cellar, lay it right on the stone-
floor, or, better yet, hang it up. An excellent way

TO KEEP FISH

is by freezing them, but here it must be remembered
that frozen fish lose much of their flavor, and when
thawed, spoil in an astonishingly short period. Where
fish are to be kept over for the next day, in the
summer-time, it is advisable to sprinkle a little salt
over them.

This, of course, applies only to localities where
fish can be obtained alive. In most cities, fish can
only be bought dead ; and in such cases, the condition of the dead fish, without regard to the manner
in which it was killed, comes into consideration. To
be able to

SELECT THE BEST

of two or more fish of the same variety, is quite
easy to learn. First of all to be considered, is the
color of the fish. This should be bright, and the
markings peculiar to the variety distinct; the gills
clean and bright red; the eyes not sunken nor pro-
truding, but they should be full and clear. If the
brilliant coloring has left the fish, it is a sign that it
has been dead for some time. This faded color does
not indicate, however, that the fish is

UNFIT FOR THE KITCHEN;

for if fish is frozen, it loses its bright color also. A fish should be firm and elastic to the touch; if you can máke an impression on it with your finger and this impression remains, it is a bad sign—it means that decay has set in. As to

THE SIZE OF FISH

best for culinary purposes, there is no rule; this is, for the greater part, regulated by individual taste. As a rule, larger fish have firmer meat. The growth of fish is not regulated by time; it depends entirely on their food-supply—the variety and the lesser or greater voracity of the individual. Fish from large bodies of clear water, in which aquatic plants abound, have a superior flavor, caused by the liberal supply of oxygen through the action of the sunlight, the quality of the food and the greater exercise ; while on the other hand, fish from a small, muddy, not to say filthy pond, have a disagreeable taste.

THE SEASON OF THE YEAR

is also of importance to the condition of fish-meat, as no fish is good during or right after its spawning-time; and, to some extent also, the sex, the males being considered of finer flavor. Regarding the selection of

THE PROPER VARIETIES,

we advise our readers to make it a rule to obtain their supplies of fish only from responsible dealers, where they are sure that no inferior variety is sold under a distinguished name, which is too often practiced, especially by peddlers. We have often wondered why the people have stood this outrage so long without a move to obtain their rights. Maybe it is because too little attention has been paid to fish all along. How could it be possible otherwise that common Suckers, fish of very little value, are frequently sold under the name of Lake Salmon, fish of a high reputation, if the venders were not aware of the ignorance of their customers. We are sure that there are few, if any, ladies in this country to whom a dry goods merchant could sell velveteen for silk velvet; need I to state why? Now, let us exercise the same judgment in fish, and

THE FRAUDULENT DEALER

will have a poor show. Besides swindling you by selling fish under a false name, such a fishdealer is also trespassing against science by injuring the reputation of a good variety of fish, which to ascertain and establish for the welfare of the people, by scientific researches, may have cost much time and money.

GENERAL RECIPES.

TO BOIL FISH.

FISH should be boiled in a regular fish-kettle. Such a kettle is oblong in shape and furnished with a double perforated tin-bottom, to which, on each end, long wire-handles are attached. Take this perforated bottom from the kettle, lay the fish you want to boil on it, add the spice, and then return all gently to the pot. The water should just cover the fish. Fish should never come to a real boiling; as soon as the water boils up once, move the kettle from the strong fire and let it only simmer for a while, according to the size of the fish; not longer than ten minutes to each pound of fish, however. When done, lift the perforated bottom by its wire-handles carefully from the water and gently slide the fish on a plate. The fish, having retained its shape this way, presents an appetizing appearance when served. Fish should always be served as soon as done. Besides using the fish-kettle for fish, it may also be used with advantage to boil hams.

TO BOIL SEAFISH.

All seafish are put on the fire with cold water; to the water add one onion, spice and one bayleaf; also, plenty of salt. Where obtainable, sea-water may be used, as this will improve the flavor of the fish. As soon as the water boils, move the kettle from the fire and set it on the back part of the stove to simmer slowly for a quarter of an hour or more, according to the size of the fish. If a seafish actually boils, it falls to pieces, and also loses its flavor.

TO BOIL FISH IN BEER.

Scale the fish, clean and wash them; also, trim their fins. Cut into pieces, if the fish are of large size; also, split them. Now lay them on a colander, and then wipe dry with a towel. In a stew-pan, put black pepper, onions (whole), sliced lemon, bayleaves, cloves, some brown crust of rye-bread and a piece of German "pfefferkuchen," and some butter. Now put the fish in, and pour "weiss"-beer or "braun"-beer (small-beer, not lager-beer!) over them in sufficient quantity to cover the fish well. Boil quickly and skim. Now melt some butter, to this add some flour, brown it slightly and add to the sauce. When the fish are done, take them out of the pot carefully with a strainer, and let the sauce boil well for quite a while yet; then add one glass of white wine, some sugar, and one teaspoonful of extract of beef. Stir well; then pour over the fish, using a strainer, and serve with boiled potatoes. Garnish with sliced lemon.

The varieties best adapted for this mode of cooking are the Lake Whitefish, River Sheepshead (White Perch), German Carp, Buffalo, Yellow Perch, and the Eel.

TO BOIL FISH IN FAT.

The most suitable for this mode of cooking fish is beef-suet, but mutton-suet or lard may also be used. Butter is not suitable, however. Put the suet or lard into a deep stew-pan and heat it to boiling; it must be so hot that when a piece of fish is dipped into it, it must turn brown immediately. The fish are scaled, cleaned, and along their sides, in distances of about two finger-widths, they are crimped (*i. e.*, little transverse cuts are made into the flesh about one-half an inch deep); or, if the fish are of a large size, they are cut into suitable pieces. The fish are then wiped with a towel and some flour strewn over them. Now beat up one or more raw eggs, dip the fish in it, and then roll in crushed bread or crackers. The fish is now ready for the pan. The pieces are laid into the hot fat in a manner so they do not touch each other. They soon rise to the top, where they brown. When completed, remove with a strainer; place on a colander to allow the grease to run off, and salt slightly on both sides. After the grease has run off, the fish is laid on a hot plate uncovered. Serve immediately after with hot butter or lemon-juice; garnish with parsley, which has been dipped in the hot grease to make it crisp. As the fat or lard can be used several times again, if care is taken not to burn it, this is not a costly way of preparing fish for the table.

Especially well adapted for this method are the Sunfish, Straw Bass, little Catfish, Smelt and Flounders; in fact, all the small varieties of fish. They become so crisp that they may be eaten with fins and bones.

BAKED OR STUFFED FISH.

Clean and scale a fish of about five pounds, then rub into it one tablespoonful of salt; mash five crackers very fine; add one tablespoonful of chopped parsley, one tablespoonful of chopped salt-pork or bacon, half a teaspoonful of ground pepper, half a tablespoonful of salt, and sufficient water to make

it into a paste. Put this inside the fish and close
it with a few stitches. Now cut gashes across the
fish about one-half an inch deep and over one inch
in length, and fill these up with strips of fat pork.
The fish is now put in a pan, sprinkled well with
pepper, salt and flour, and adding hot water enough
to cover the bottom of the pan, it is set in a hot
oven to bake.

Bake one hour, repeatedly pouring its gravy over
the fish, and adding hot water as often as necessary
to keep the bottom of the pan covered. When done,
place on a large dish and garnish with parsley or celery; serve with Holland sauce.

For a pan in which fish are to be baked, it is
also advisable to have a perforated second bottom,
like the one used in the fish-kettle; fish are much
easier to handle with its aid.

The above method applies especially to large fish
or varieties that have dry flesh, such as Buffalo,
Muskalonge, Pike and large Carp.

FISH PUDDING.

Take three pounds of fish, scale and skin, clean
and unbone; chop fine, with some parsley and one
onion. Take one-quarter of a pound of butter,
beat to a foam; then add, one at a time, six eggs,
stirring well; now add the chopped fish, and pour

over all this, very little at a time, under continuous stirring which should last about one-half an hour, about one quart of milk; then add a handful of grated bread, a good dose of salt and some grated nutmeg. Put in a well-buttered mold and bake one hour in the oven. Serve with water-cress, well mixed with sweet oil, vinegar, pepper, salt, and boiled beets cut into small, square pieces. The following sauce may be substituted: Take a handful of morcheln (morels, a kind of mushroom), blanche it, squeeze well with both hands and chop fine; roast a spoonful of flour in some butter to a light yellow; simmer the morcheln with some chopped parsley, to this add half a pint of bouillon and season with salt and nutmeg.

FISH PIE.

Make a short dough and roll it to the thickness of a straw; butter the holes of an egg-pan and line each hole singly with this dough; then fill them with dry peas and bake to a light brown. Remove the peas when done. Take boiled, baked or fried fish, remnants will do, pick into small pieces, add a couple of spoonfuls of white sauce, to which may be added a few capers; put this into a small stew-pan and heat in hot water; then fill into the hot pastry.

FISH RAGOUT.

After a fish has been well washed and wiped dry again, free it of its skin and bones; then cut it up into small, square pieces, salt it, and stew over a gentle fire in butter and lemon-juice. When done place on a colander, to free it from its liquor. Now make a stiff sauce of flour, butter, salt, bouillon and one teaspoonful of extract of beef; then add the yolks of two raw eggs and some sardelle butter; mix all this carefully with the fish, taking care not to break the latter; fill in large, scalloped shells; sprinkle with crushed bread and Parmesan cheese, and place a small piece of butter on top of each shellful of ragout; set in the oven and bake to a light brown.

FISH SALAD.

Take fish that were boiled in salt-water or fried, remnants will answer, and carefully clean of skin and bones, taking care not to mash the meat. Take the yolks of three hard-boiled eggs and rub them very fine; then slowly add the yolks of three raw eggs and a little salt. After stirring this for quite a while, add, by drops, one-quarter of a pound of sweet oil, some sharp vinegar or lemon-juice, and one teaspoonful of extract of beef. Then add the fish, together with a couple of teaspoonfuls of capers, and mix carefully.

See also special recipé of Russian salad

FISH SOUPS.

See the special recipés.

FISH SÜLZE.

Take either fresh-water or sea fish, clean and cut into pieces, salt well and pour hot vinegar over it. Boil some white wine, water and a little vinegar with slices of lemon, whole pepper, cloves, mace, bayleaves and salt ; put the fish into it and simmer until done, then take the fish out again and sprinkle it with vinegar and lemon-juice. Strain the sauce through a cloth or hair sieve ; add a little gelatine ; place the fish nicely in layers in a mold and pour the sauce over it, to cover, and set in a cool place. When wanted on the table, reverse the mold on a plate and serve with vinegar, oil, mustard and sugar ; with salad, or a sharp sauce like the following : Chop two dozen juniper berries very fine, take the yolks of four hard-boiled eggs and rub them through a sieve, one tablespoonful of sugar, three of mustard, six of sweet oil, three of white wine vinegar, and half a glassful of red wine, and mix well together. The juniper berries may be left out.

CURRY POWDER.

This desirable spice is used very extensively for various dishes, and forms an important part in preparing certain fishes. In the following, we offer the true recipé for mixing it. Take by weight

Curcuma, ...	8 parts.
Coriander, ...	8 "
Black Pepper, ...	5 "
Ginger, ...	3⅜ "
Cinnamon, ...	1 "
Mace, ...	1 "
Cloves, ...	1 "
Cardamon, ...	2 "
Caraway, ...	½ "
Cayenne Pepper, ...	2 "

These spices are dried in an oven, and then pulverized in a mortar and well mixed. Keep in an airtight jar.

SPECIAL RECIPES.

———

THE foregoing recipés for preparing fish in different styles for the table are general; those that now follow are epicurean specialties, either of localities or nations, best suited for certain varieties of fish, etc. Those marked with an asterisk (*) are added by the author.

BASS, WITH CAPER-SAUCE.*

A Black Bass, Rock Bass (Goggle Eye) or a Yellow Perch is scaled and cleaned, crimped on the sides and washed. Put in the kettle, with water to cover. In the water with the fish put salt, black pepper (whole) and onions; cook slowly, about six minutes to each pound of fish, and take out of the kettle when done. Now melt butter and flour, yellow, and add finely chopped onions; then a little of the fish-water out of the kettle, some water and fresh butter; then sliced lemon, and, last, some capers. The latter must not be allowed to boil, as this would spoil their flavor.

(20)

BLACK BASS, with Butter.*

Select fish that each weigh two pounds and upward, scale, clean, crimp and wash. The heads are to be left on the fish. Boil in salt-water, with small whole onions and whole black pepper, until done. Take some butter, heat it but do not brown it, and add, while on the fire, some finely chopped parsley. Put the fish on a plate, pour this butter-sauce over it, garnish with sprigs of parsley, and serve with boiled potatoes.

BASS, Fried.*

The fish are scaled, cleaned and crimped, then salted, and left thus for a little while. The fish are then rolled in beaten eggs and crushed bread or crackers, and fried in hot lard, brown on both sides. Yellow Perch and small Catfish may be treated the same way.

STRAW BASS (Rock Bass, Crappie, etc.).*

These flat fish, including also the Sunfish, may be fried after the manner given under the general recipé, but they may also be boiled after the general rule; in this case, take, when the fish are nearly done, two tablespoonfuls of flour, stir into melted butter, to this add a tablespoonful of chopped parsley, put into the kettle with the fish, and simmer until the fish is done.

BUFFALO, Baked.*

After the fish is scaled, split and cut into pieces, salt it, and let it lie thus for an hour; then wipe dry and roll in beaten eggs, and then in crushed bread. Take half lard and half butter, brown it, then lay the fish in it and bake to a light brown on both sides. Use the gravy, left from baking, to go with the fish. Serve with boiled potatoes or potato salad. German Carp may be baked in the same manner. See also stuffed fish.

BULLFROGS.*

Kill the Frogs with a cut across their heads. Take the hind-quarters and part of the back, skin them and sprinkle with salt and pepper; then roll in beaten eggs and crushed bread, and fry to a light brown. Serve with toasts. This is a delicious dish.

AMERICAN CARP.*

These are boiled in water with spice and one onion; when done, melt some good butter, in which stir some flour; then add a little nutmeg, a couple of spoonfuls of fish-water, and stir all this to a sauce; now add the yolk of a raw egg, and season with lemon-juice to taste. Mullet may be cooked the same way.

GERMAN CARP (Silesian style).

Let the Carp bleed freely when you have killed it; scale it and remove the intestines. Now take a sharp knife and make along its back, from the head to the tail, two parallel cuts into the skin, each about one-half an inch apart; salt the fish and let it remain so for half an hour. Then cut bacon, a lemon and salt sardelles into narrow strips of about one and one-half inches in length. Wash the fish and draw, with the aid of a carding-needle, these little pieces of bacon, lemon and sardelle alternately and crosswise through that part of the fish's back that lies between the two parallel cuts. Instead of bacon, one may substitute sliced pickles. Now put some butter in a pan; when this is melted and yellow, lay the Carp gently in it and bake for half an hour; then add a glassful of wine and some good beef-juice to the gravy, and bake five minutes longer. Then serve. It may here be added that Carp of three pounds and more are the best for the table, and Mirror or Leather Carp best adapted for this mode of preparing it.

GERMAN CARP, with Sardelles.

The Carp is scaled, split, cut into pieces and washed quickly; then salt well, and leave it so for an hour. Now put some butter in a sauce-pan; on this a layer of Carp-pieces, which have been well wiped, and on this some capers; then well-soaked and unboned sardelles; again butter, which, in turn, is followed by fish, and so on; the topmost layer must be capers, sardelles and butter. Over all this pour a glassful of wine and the juice of half a lemon, and let it simmer for half an hour. Serve the Carp on a plate with its own sauce, and potatoes.

When *wine* is mentioned, it refers to any of our light native wines.

GERMAN CARP, Blue (Prussian style).

The most suitable for this dish is the Scale Carp. Care must be taken that the fish loses none of the slime that covers its scales; the scales are left on the fish. Kill the fish as directed in the Introduction; remove the intestines, and cut the fish, if necessary, into pieces. Now color it blue by pouring boiling vinegar over it, and then boil in salt-water, to which some spice is added. Serve with a sauce made of equal parts of grated horse-radish and apples, mixed with vinegar, sugar and salt. Remoulade sauce also goes well with this dish. See Sauces.

GERMAN CARP, in Beer (Saxon style).*

Take a Scale Carp of three or four pounds in weight; as soon as it is killed, cut it open, remove the intestines, and rinse the inside with a little **vin**-egar ; this you save, as also the blood. The intes-tines, excepting the gall, air-bladder and stomach, are tied into a little bundle and remain with the fish. The fish is neither scaled nor wiped. On the bottom of the kettle lay one sliced carrot, one small celeriac (turnip-rooted celery)—sliced, about eight medium-sized onions—whole, a tablespoonful of salt, some black pepper—whole, cloves, six bayleaves, some rye-bread crust, allspice, one-half a lemon and one-half a pound of butter. Now cut the fish into six or eight pieces, including the head, and also lay in the kettle—the little bundle with the intestines, and the roe, put in the center of it ; barely cover the fish with "weiss" or "braun" beer (small-beer), and put on the fire. As soon as it begins to boil, look at the clock, for it has to boil slowly just three-quarters of an hour; and add another half pound, or less, of butter. When nearly done, add the vinegar with the blood, and a small piece of German "pfeffer-kuchen" dissolved in a little beer, to season the sauce. Serve with boiled potatoes as soon as done ; the sauce is used as it leaves the kettle, not strained.

BAKED GERMAN CARP.

(See Buffalo.)

MOCK CAVIAR.

Two or three Dutch Herrings are cleaned and soaked in water for a couple of hours, then laid in lukewarm milk for five hours; now skin and unbone them, chop very fine, and mix with finely chopped onions and the juice of a lemon. Serve with bread • and fresh butter.

CATFISH.*

See stuffed fish; also Bass, fried, and Eel in jelly.

CLAM CHOWDER (Long Island style).*

Take fifty clams, one pound of veal, one-half pound of bacon, one pint of milk, some water, six crackers, one teaspoonful each of thyme and sweet marjoram, one teaspoonful of chopped parsley, one onion, three potatoes, and salt and pepper to taste. Line the bottom of the sauce-pan with the bacon cut into pieces; pare and cut the potatoes into small pieces, chop the onion fine, cut the veal into small pieces, chop the clams and mash the crackers. Now put a layer of potatoes on the bacon, and then sprinkle some onion, marjoram, parsley, salt and pepper over this; then make a layer of veal, then one of chopped clams, and keep on until all is in the sauce-pan, arranging, however, that the last layer will be clams. Now add boiling water to the whole, but not more than to just cover it; cover well, place on a slow fire and simmer for half an hour without stirring; then add the milk and crushed crackers, stir and cook a few minutes longer, and then serve. If preferred, one or more tomatoes may be-added.

CODFISH, Fried.
(See also Haddock.)

For five or six persons, take four pounds of fresh Codfish, cut in slices of the thickness of a finger, pepper and salt well on both sides, then set aside for a little while; now roll the fish in flour or beaten eggs and crushed bread, and fry slowly in butter, or half lard and half butter, to a light brown on both sides. Serve with boiled kale, parsnip or cabbage, or alone with grated horse-radish and vinegar, or brown sauce. See Sauces.

CODFISH, Boiled.

Take one and one-half pounds of dried Codfish for five persons. The fish, after being well beaten with a mallet, is soaked for thirty-six hours in water to which a little soda is added; change this water once every three hours. Skin the fish and cut into suitable pieces. Put the stew-pot with water on the fire, adding a couple of onions cut into quarters; when to a boiling-point, place the fish in it and wait until it boils again, when it should be taken from the fire at once and left to draw for five minutes longer. Take out of the pot, place on a colander, salt it and then put on a plate. Serve with browned butter and mustard.

CODFISH BALLS (Virginia style).*

One pound of Codfish, one and one-half pounds of mashed potatoes, two spoonfuls of good butter and the yolks of two fresh eggs. Skin and unbone the fish, then weigh and soak over night; in the morning change the water, and pour over it enough hot water to cover it. Let it stand on the range where it will keep warm for about ten minutes; then change the water again, and let it boil ten minutes. Take the fish out, pick and chop it very fine; mash the potatoes while hot and mix with the fish; add the butter and yolks of the eggs, into which you have previously stirred half a teaspoonful of mixed mustard. Make into small, round balls and fry a nice brown in butter and lard mixed.

TO BOIL CRABS OR CRAWFISH.
(See also Lobster.)

Set the pot or kettle with water on a hot fire, and add some caraway, salt and green parsley. Wash the crabs clean. When the water boils, put in the crabs, also a piece of butter, and let it boil one-quarter of an hour longer; then serve.

SOFT-SHELLED CRABS.*
(Fulton Market style.)

Lift the shell of the crabs and remove the spongy substance on both sides; then put your thumb-nail under the so-called apron—this is the tail, which is pressed close against the lower part of the body—and pull it off; also, cut off the ends of the legs. Do not wash nor scald them, as this will injure their flavor—simply wipe them clean; then dip in beaten eggs and roll in crushed bread which has been well seasoned with pepper and salt, and fry in boiling lard or oil for about ten minutes. Garnish with parsley and lemons cut in quarters.

EEL, Baked.

Cut the Eel in pieces, season with salt and pepper, and let them lie thus for a couple of hours; then dry them with a towel, roll in beaten eggs, then in crushed bread or crackers, and bake brown on both sides. Serve with Remoulade sauce.

EEL, in JELLY.

Middle-sized Eels are killed by a cut across their heads, and then salted and freed of all their slime; then cut them into pieces, these put in a pot, and boil in water with bayleaves, spice, plenty of salt and finely chopped onions until tender; while boiling, add about a teacupful of vinegar to the water. The pieces of Eel are now taken from the pot and the water still allowed to boil for quite a while, until it shows signs of thickening. In the meantime, the pieces of Eel are arranged nicely in a tin-mold with some slices of lemon; the sauce is then poured through a strainer over the pieces into the mold, and left to get cold and stiff. Serve with olive oil and vinegar. Tench or Catfish may be substituted.

PICKLED EEL.

Clean the Eels well, inside and outside, with water; then let them lie for about one hour in salt; now wipe them dry with a towel, cut into pieces, and fry in a very clean frying-pan in olive oil; when done, lay the pieces on blotting-paper to cool off. To the oil that remains in the pan, add a little white pepper, mace (whole), some bayleaves, sliced lemon and some challottes; also, a sufficient quantity of vinegar and water as will cover all the pieces of Eel when put into a vessel; let this sauce boil for about fifteen or twenty minutes. The pieces of Eel are now placed in jars or stone crocks, and the sauce, after it has cooled off, is poured over them to cover the same about one-half an inch; the vessels are then closed air-tight, and set away in a cool but dry place. Eel thus treated keeps for a great length of time.

EEL, with Sage.

Kill the Eel, wipe with salt, cut into pieces and wash well. Cut one onion in slices, add allspice, bayleaf, pepper, some vinegar and sage; put into a stew-pot, together with the Eel, and cover with water; now add plenty of salt; boil over a quick fire until done. The sauce is made by adding some fresh butter and flour to the fish-water. Serve with potatoes boiled in the skin (unpared) and cucumber salad.

See also Pike with Eel.

EEL SOUP (Hamburg style).
(See Soups.)

EELPOUT, Blue.

After the fish is cleaned, salt it freely; then pour boiling vinegar over it and let it stand in this, frequently turning it over, for one hour; now boil in salt-water, with onion and spice. Serve with caper-sauce or the following horse-radish sauce: Three spoonfuls of sweet cream, three of vinegar, one of sugar and three of grated horse-radish; mix well, then serve.

EELPOUT, Sour.

Clean the fish well and cut into pieces; boil as above, and skim well. Take bacon, cut it into pieces and render it; to these add chopped onions, some flour, ground pepper, vinegar, and a little sugar and sugar-color; pour all this over the fish in the pot, and let it boil up once; then serve.

FLOUNDER, Green.

Clean the fish, cut in pieces and salt it. In a flat sauce-pan, simmer chopped onions and parsley roots in water, and add to this some butter and half a teaspoonful of ground pepper; put the fish in this sauce, add a sufficient quantity of water to cover the fish, cover well and simmer until done. Now take the fish out, and add to the fish-water one spoonful of flour, one of butter and one of finely chopped parsley; boil this for a minute or two, and serve with the fish.

FLOUNDERS AND SOLES, Fried or Broiled.

These are rolled in beaten eggs, then in flour and salt, and fried in butter. They may also be salted for twenty-four hours, then washed and dried in the wind, to be broiled over the fire when wanted.

LARGE FLOUNDERS OR FLATFISH.

Clean and scrape the fish, then cut into nice pieces, wash and salt them. Put a plate on the bottom of the stew-pot, and on this lay the pieces; then add one-half a pint of sharp vinegar, but *no water*. Let the pieces boil in these vinegar fumes over a hot fire; then serve with hot butter, mustard and chopped parsley, which is mixed with the vinegar in which the fish was cooked.

See also Soles and Turbot.

FISH BALLS.
(See Codfish.)

FISH, in Jelly.
(See Eel; also, Fish Sülze.)

GARFISH.*

Gars, or Garpikes as some call them, are a great dish to many people, and, as the fishermen along the Ohio inform us, the demand for this fish for the kitchen is on the increase. To dress a Gar, chop off its head and tail, cut its belly open, clean and skin it. It is said to be good either way, boiled or baked.

HADDOCK, Stewed.

Split the fish, skin and unbone it; then cut it into pieces, and treat like fried Codfish. Pare one quart of potatoes, cut into thick slices, and boil together with chopped parsley roots until almost done. Now arrange the fish and these potatoes in layers in a shallow sauce-pan, cover well and simmer until done; then add some finely chopped green parsley; thicken the sauce with one spoonful of flour and one of butter, let this boil for a minute ; then serve.

HADDOCK, with Sardelle Sauce.

Prepare the fish in the same manner as directed for fried Codfish. In a stew-pot put chopped onions and chopped parsley roots; simmer for a while, then add the fish, and fill up with water to barely cover the fish ; cover well and simmer until done. To the fish-water add one-half a spoonful of flour, one spoonful of butter, two or three finely chopped sardelles, one teaspoonful of good vinegar, then stir the yolks of two fresh eggs in it and let it come to boiling once more; then serve.

HAKE, with Parsley.

Clean and wash well. Put on the fire with cold water, to which add parsley roots and foliage, and one bayleaf. When done, garnish with the same parsley, and pour some of the fish-water on the plate.

FRESH HERRINGS.

These may be fried or boiled, following the general recipés. If to be boiled, use allspice instead of black pepper, for seasoning. Serve with oil and vinegar.

HERRING, WITH BROWN SAUCE.

Clean, then salt the Herring and wipe dry ; roll in flour and grated bread, and fry in butter or lard. Serve with the following sauce: Take a medium-sized onion, one-quarter of a pound of lean bacon, some ground pepper, one tablespoonful of flour and two of good white wine vinegar ; chop the onion, cut the bacon in small, square pieces, and simmer till the bacon is soft; now add the flour, then half a quart of water (fish-water, if you have any), and boil to a short, brownish sauce.

ROAST HERRINGS, PICKLED.

Fresh Herrings are cleaned and washed, then soaked for twelve hours in vinegar, to which onions, bayleaves and allspice are added. They are then taken out and fried in butter, brown on both sides : this done, they are placed in a tureen and the same vinegar poured over them again.

SMOKED HERRINGS, Fried.

The fish are opened and soaked for twelve hours in warm milk; then wipe dry and fry in butter or oil until the skin bursts. Serve with oil or butter and toasts.

SMOKED HERRING, à la Dauphin.

(Mr. Carême's style.)

Skin and unbone the fish, then soak half an hour in warm milk. Taken out of this, it is wiped dry and tipped in a sauce of melted sweet butter, some yolks of fresh eggs and finely chopped shives, and fried with some browned flour in a skillet. Serve with toasted bread, on which some cayenne pepper is sprinkled.

SMOKED HERRING, à l' Italienne.

The fish is well cleaned and washed in boiling water, then dried, and inside and outside dredged with flour. Fry in oil, to which some chopped parsley is added, and serve with maccaroni.

SMOKED HERRING, as Bishop's Ragout.

Five or six smoked Herrings are cut in pieces, without being washed or soaked, and fried in lard; when done, add some finely chopped leek. Serve with mashed potatoes and shives.

SMOKED HERRING, à la St. Menehould.

In a skillet put some butter, one spoonful of flour, one cupful of milk, bayleaves, thyme and pepper. Skin and open the Herring and boil it in this; then dry it again and let it cool off, dredge with butter and flour and fry done. Beat the yolks of fresh eggs, add chopped parsley, oil and lemon-juice, and serve with the fish.

SMOKED HERRING, in Butter-Paste.

Split the Herring, remove the spinal column, then wash in milk. When dried, again lay in fish-farce, to which some parsley and challottes are added. Each piece of fish is then covered with dough in such a manner that the shape of the fish remains; then baste with beaten egg and bake in an oven.

SMOKED HERRING, in Oil.

Freed of skin and bones, wash the fish in boiling water, dry and cool it off; now stick whole cloves into the meat of the fish, and place it in sweet oil. Serve with bread and butter.

SMOKED HERRING, with Onions.

The fish is cleaned, then soaked for some time in water and dried again; cut some onions in slices and fry with the fish. Serve with hot butter, to which some mustard is added.

SMOKED HERRING (Scottish style).

Clean the fish, and, if they are dry in meat, pour some warm beer or water over them; when dry again, fry in oil or sweet butter. Serve with hot or cold butter, mashed potatoes or parsnips.

See also Smoked Fish.

LOBSTERS.

These are washed clean, then boiled in salt-water from one-half to three-quarters of an hour, according to their size. If wanted cold, let them cool off in the water.

CANNED LOBSTERS AND LOBSTER SALAD.

Recipés for preparing these being, as a rule, on the cans, we omit them here.

FRESH MACKEREL, BOILED.

Clean and wash, boil whole or cut in pieces in water and salt. Serve with hot butter and parsley or mustard and butter.

FRIED MACKEREL.

Split the fish after it is cleaned and soak in salt-water; then wrap some fresh fennel around it and fry in oil, to which salt, pepper and dry fennel are added. Serve with a sauce of brown butter, finely chopped herbs, nutmeg, salt, fennel, capers and wine vinegar.

MACKEREL, WITH OYSTERS.

Clean, wash and cut into nice pieces, then boil in white wine, to which add some water, salt and herbs. Serve with Oyster sauce.

SPANISH MACKEREL, BROILED.*

Split the Mackerel down the back, rub over it some butter or salad oil, and then sprinkle it with salt and pepper. Put it on the gridiron before a good fire and brown on both sides; when done, squeeze lemon-juice on it and garnish with sprays of parsley.

MULLET.

(See American Carp.)

TO BOIL MUSSELS.

Clean the Mussels well in cold, fresh water, and remove those that should open while washed; put in boiling water and boil with salt, onions and whole pepper until they begin to open. Take out with a strainer and serve hot.

OYSTERS, Fried (Baltimore style).*

Drain the Oysters thoroughly in a colander. Cover a board well with cracker-dust (pounded crackers), and on this place the Oysters in two straight rows (handle the Oysters carefully with your fingers, use no fork); when they have soaked about one-quarter of an hour, place those of the row nearest to you, one by one, on top of those on the upper row, in such a manner that the cracker-dust of the one comes between the two, and the thick parts of both form the two ends. This done, sprinkle again with cracker-dust and wait another quarter of an hour for it to soak. Now take each couple nicely between your hands and press them gently into an oblong shape, using plenty of cracker-dust to keep your hands dry, and lay them carefully in a skillet with boiling, hot lard, and fry brown and crisp on both sides. Serve immediately when done, with crackers, pickles, tomato catsup, pepper and salt. Oysters may be crackered and shaped hours before they are used, but they will lose in flavor and appearance if fried ahead.

OYSTER STEW (Baltimore style).*

Put the Oysters with their liquor in a sauce-pan on the fire; heat, but do not boil; now pour the liquor off into another sauce-pan and set on the fire;

as soon as it boils up in this, add some fresh butter, pepper and salt to taste, one-half pint of boiled, hot milk, and, when to a boiling again, add the Oysters and take from the fire at once. If preferred, some cracker-dust or flour may be added to the milk to thicken the liquor. When ready to serve, put a small piece of butter on each plate and pour the stew over it.

YELLOW PERCH.*

(See Bass; also, Fish in Beer and Fried Fish.)

WHITE PERCH.

(See Sheepshead.)

PIKE PERCH, in Holland style.

This fish is known under a great many different names. It is also called Wall-eyed Pike, Glass-eye, Gray Pike, Ohio Salmon, etc.

Scale and clean a fine specimen, trim its fins, salt it in and outside and let it lie thus for several hours. One hour before the fish is to be served put on the fire in cold water, to which salt and some milk are added. When near boiling remove from the hot fire and simmer until done. Take it carefully out, slide it on an oblong hot plate; put its liver, which was boiled with the fish, together with a bunch of parsley in its mouth and garnish with the following: Selected small potatoes are pared, boiled, then fried, whole; several eggs are boiled hard—when cold chop coarsely, the white and the yolks alone; then chop, also coarse, some parsley. Now arrange a ring of the potatoes close around the fish, then one of the yellow, next one of the white, and near the edge of the plate finish with a green border.

PIKE PERCH, Boiled.

Take a large fish, scale, clean and crimp it along its back; wash it, then salt it well and let it remain so for one hour. Then take the fish and bend it by means of a string, which is passed through its eyes and fastened to its tail, to a nice circle and wash it again. Put into the kettle and boil with plenty of salt and onions. For sauce, simmer some flour in butter, add some finely chopped chalottes, fish-water, mustard to taste, wine vinegar and sliced lemon, also a little sugar; let this boil five minutes. Put the fish on a plate, pour some of this sauce over the fish and serve the rest in a gravy-boat with the fish. This sauce may be substituted with brown butter and mustard.

PIKE, à la KUFFER.

A Pike, or Muskallunge, of several pounds in weight is crimped (gashes cut into it) along its entire length, well peppered and salted, wrapped in a large sheet of paper, placed on a tin-pan in an oven and baked carefully for half an hour. When done take the paper off, put on a plate and serve.

PIKE, in Baden style.

A Pike is cleaned and opened from head to tail, then unboned, salted and wiped dry. Place in a long earthen bake-pan, dredge with pepper. Put a small chopped onion and some butter in a stew-pan, simmer yellow and pour this over the entire length of the fish; this done, pour a pint of sour cream over it in the same manner, then dredge with a quarter of a pound of grated Parmesan cheese and some grated bread. Bake one quarter of an hour to a nice yellow. Serve with its own gravy.

PIKE OR PICKEREL FRIED.*

Take fish that weigh less than three-quarters of a pound. Clean and scale, but leave their fins on, then crimp slightly and salt. After letting them lie thus for a while, wipe dry and cut their heads off; then roll in beaten egg, next in flour mixed with a

little grated bread and fry in butter on both sides.
To the butter that remains in the killet add some hot
bouillon, vinegar or lemon-juice, and serve with the
fish, or serve with hot butter and chopped parsley.

LARDED PIKE.

A large Pike is cleaned and scaled and larded with
fat bacon. Put in a pan with plenty of butter and
bake, basting well and often; when almost done
dredge with grated bread and cream.

See also Stuffed Fish.

PIKE, WITH HORSE-RADISH.

The fish is boiled with onions, salt and pepper;
when done place on a hot plate and dredge with
grated horse-radish. Make some butter very hot
(screeching) and pour over the horse-radish on the
fish to curl it.

PIKE, WITH EEL.

(Stettin style.)

Select a medium-sized Pike and a large Eel, cut
them in pieces and wash all the blood off. Lay part
of the Pike in a tined stew-pan, then the Eel, over
this scatter chopped onions and then add the rest of
the Pike; add salt and water and place on the fire to
boil. Skim well. Take butter, hot flour, grated

nutmeg, a little pepper and finely chopped sardelles, mixed well together and add with some sliced lemon to the fish when nearly done. Put on a plate, sprinkle some capers over the fish and serve.

RED SNAPPER, Boiled.*

Clean, wash and wipe the fish, then rub the juice of a lemon into it and sprinkle with pepper and salt. Put into a cloth, then into the kettle, cover with hot water and salt well. Let it boil gently, skimming carefully. If lemons are not at hand add one-half pint of vinegar to the water when the fish is put in the kettle. Put on a hot plate and garnish with parsley and sliced lemons.

RED SNAPPER, Baked.
(See Baked Fish.)

RUSSIAN SALAD.*

Take a quarter of a pound of cold roast veal, the same amount of Salamie sausage, six cold boiled potatoes (boiled in their skin), one nice apple, one good-sized onion, one boiled red beet and three cucumber pickles; cut all of this into little strips, as much as possible, of a uniform size and put it in a large bowl. Now take a clean, well-watered male Dutch Herring, unbone it and also cut it, including the milt, in small strips and add to the balance; this done, take a small bowl, drop the yolk of a fresh egg in it, add a pinch of salt, and under continuous stirring add, carefully and alternately, very little at a time, mixed French mustard and olive oil, until about one tablespoonful of mustard and three of oil are thus mixed with the egg; pour this mayonnaise over the salad, add one tablespoonful of capers and mix well together. Then heap it upon a flat plate and decorate artistically with pickles, hard-boiled eggs, sardelles, beets, lemon and parsley or celery. This salad is best if made the day before it is to be used.

MAYONNAISE.

Instead of mixed French mustard, English mustard powder may be used; in this case, mix the mustard with the egg first, then add alternately, as above, the vinegar and olive oil, beginning with the vinegar. This will make the mayonnaise of a golden color, but of a somewhat different flavor.

SALMON, à la GLASER.

Cut the fish in slices of finger-thickness, wipe each slice dry, but use no water, then pepper and salt them. Heat butter to a light yellow in a skillet, fry the pieces carefully yellow on one side, now put sliced onions in the skillet and fry the other side of the fish also yellow. Put the fish on a plate, add some hot bouillon to the butter and onions, let it come to a boil and pour over the fish, then serve.

SALMON, BOILED.

Cut the fish into slices of about one to two inches in thickness, and soak these for fifteen minutes in vinegar. If the fish is to be served warm, take, to each pound of fish, one tablespoonful of salt; if cold, put less salt in the water; in both cases, however, add one glassful of white wine, some bazil, bayleaves, cloves, whole black pepper and quartered onions. Put the fish in the kettle when the water boils. Serve —hot, with hot butter and mustard or with caper-sauce; cold, with cold fish sauce. See Sauces.

CANNED SALMON.

Recipés for this are, as a rule, on the respective cans.

SARDELLE BUTTER.

Take, by weight, equal parts of washed and un-boned Sardelles and fresh butter, mash very fine and rub through a sieve. The Sardelles may be substituted with the milt of Dutch Herrings.

BOILED SHAD, Cold.

Put water, to which some vinegar, bayleaves, a couple of onions and a small handful of salt are added, on the fire. Cut the fish into nice pieces, and place in the water as soon as it boils. When done, take the fish-kettle from the fire and let the fish cool off while in the water.

BOILED SHAD, Warm.

Clean the fish, but do not cut it in pieces. Put plain salt-water on the fire; as soon as it boils, put the fish in it, but as soon as it boils again, take from the fire and simmer until done. Serve with boiled potatoes and hot butter.

SHAD, in Claret or Beer.

Scale the fish and wash well; then cut it open and remove the intestines, taking care not to injure the gall bladder; save the liver and the roe. Now cut the fish into nice pieces, but wash it no more, to save the blood. In a bowl place two sliced onions, one sliced lemon, two pieces of ginger, two bayleaves, six or eight cloves; rub some salt over the fish and place it with the liver, and the roe on top of it. Over this pour one pint of red wine or small-beer, and let it soak two hours in a cool place; then boil it all gently in a well-glazed pot, with an addition of a little sugar and one tablespoonful of butter. If desired, the sauce may be made thicker by adding some flour when done. Serve hot or cold with this sauce.

SMELT, Fried.

Salt the Smelts and then wipe them dry, roll in flour or in beaten egg and crushed bread, fry in very hot fat to a nice yellow, and serve with kale or alone with toast.

SMELT, Sour.

Boil a couple of onions, some herbs, spice and caraway with water; then strain it, and add to the water some salt and vinegar; put the Smelts in it and boil six or eight minutes. For sauce, cut one-quarter of a pound of bacon and some onions in little, square pieces, and roast these to a light brown; then add a spoonful of flour and boil it with some vinegar, salt, fish-water and sugar until it thickens; mix with the Smelts and serve.

SMOKED FISH, with Cerealine.*

Take two *so-called* Lake Herrings—for they are, in reality, young Whitefish, and only resemble a Herring in size and color—cut off their heads and tails, skin and unbone, then fry with good butter in a skillet. Take two and one-half cupfuls of cerealine flakes, to this add two cupfuls of cold water, and set it aside a few minutes to soak; then boil it slowly for eight or ten minutes, stirring well, over a moderate fire; add one tablespoonful of good butter and season with pepper, salt and nutmeg; then remove it from the fire, but keep it on the stove until you are ready to serve it with the fish.

SMOKED FISH, with Rice.

Boil one-half a pound of rice in one quart of bouillon well done; then heat four tablespoonfuls of finely chopped onions with some butter and six mashed white pepper-seeds; this, with an additional teaspoonful of fresh butter, mix with the rice. Now skin and unbone two or three medium-sized smoked fish, cut them into small bites and fry a little while in butter; then butter a plate, on which place half of the rice, then the fish, and, in turn, the rest of the rice; form this into a nice pyramid, baste with beaten egg, then dredge with grated cheese and bread, add another small piece of butter, and bake in an oven—taking care that the plate does not get too hot from below.

SHEEPSHEAD.*

Is boiled like Bass, with capers or Red Snapper; it may also be baked or fried.

SALAMANDER, Baked.*

That the large Salamanders (Menopoma Alleghan-
iense) that live in our rivers and lakes are eatable
will surprise most of our readers, but it is a fact,
nevertheless. We have seen them on the bills of fare
on the most stylish epicurian banquets of New York
City.

After they are killed, by a cut through their head,
rubbed with salt, washed and wiped dry, then, dis-
emboweled, they are treated like fish. See recipé
Baked and Stuffed Fish.

SAUCES.

CELERY SAUCE.–Simmer two celery bulbs (celeriac) with butter quite done, add two cupfuls of sweet cream, stir it together and then rub it through a hair-sieve. Put it on the fire again, season to taste and heat almost to boiling, then use.

COLD FISH SAUCE.—Take the yolks of three or four hard-boiled eggs, pour some sweet oil over them, mash and stir this well; then add a teaspoonful of finely chopped challottes and some vinegar, rub it through a sieve and mix with some cold fish-water, mustard and chopped parsley.

FISH SAUCE.—Heat two tablespoonfuls of flour with one of butter, add one grated onion and mix with half a pint of fish-water, then add one tea-spoonful of Curry powder and a tablespoonful of finely chopped pickle. If this sauce is not sharp enough to one's taste, add some lemon-juice. Boil all this until it shows signs of thickening.

(52)

HOLLAND SAUCE.—Melt a piece of gooα butter in a sauce-pan, stir some flour, salt and grated nutmeg into it, and add sufficient fish-water to give you plenty of sauce. When it begins to thicken remove from the fire and stir some lemon-juice, vinegar or a glass of white wine to it, also the yolk of a fresh egg well beaten and a little cream.

MAYONAISE SAUCE.—Into a small bowl drop the clear yolks of one or two fresh eggs, add a little salt and lemon-juice and stir well together, then add olive oil by drops, under continuous stirring, and now and then, as it thickens, a few drops of Estragon vinegar. If well stirred the sauce will be quite thick, and may be thinned with bouillon or aspic; add white pepper and salt to taste.

MUSTARD SAUCE.—Heat two spoonfuls of flour in butter, add bouillon and vinegar and let it come to boiling; remove from the fire and add two spoonfuls of French mustard, a little sugar and salt.

REMOULADE SAUCE.—Make some golden-colored mayonnaise (see Russian Salad) and add sufficient French mustard to darken its color, and also some grated onions.

TARTAR SAUCE*—Is made of mayonnaise, to which finely chopped onions, pickles, parsley and capers also chopped, are added.

WHITE SAUCE.—Heat two tablespoonfuls of flour in some sweet oil, stir some good bouillon into it and let it come to boiling, then take it from the fire and, under continuous stirring, during which you add some Estragon vinegar, salt, ground white pepper, a little sugar and a few drops of lemon-juice, let it cool off.

WINE SAUCE.—Stir two tablespoonfuls of flour into some water, add two glasses of white wine, one of fish-water, salt, a piece of good butter, the yolks of four fresh eggs, and beat all this over the fire into a cream-like sauce.

SOUPS.

CLAM SOUP.*

Strain the liquor from about fifty clams and put it in a sauce-pan. Let it boil ten minutes, skimming well while boiling. Add two quarts of hot water, one quarter pound of butter and a teaspoonful of chopped parsley; then the clams, chopped fine, a pint of cream, and salt and pepper to taste. Boil five minutes longer, then serve.

EEL SOUP (Hamburg style).

Take the bone of a smoked ham, some bacon or beef, set it with plenty of water on the fire and boil it for two hours, then add green peas, some parsley roots and carrots. Clean the Eel, cut it in pieces and boil with vinegar, salt, bayleaves and pepper, done. Take a cupful of flour, the yolk of a fresh egg and water and make a dough of it. Now heat some flour in butter, stir this into the soup, let it

(55)

come to boiling again, then add the dough, cut into
small bites with a knife, vinegar, some red or white
wine and a little sugar. Put finely choped eel-grass
and parsley in a tureen, then the Eel, and over this
pour the soup and serve with preserved pears.

SOLES (Filets de Soles).

Take the four filets of the fish, salt them and
simmer for half an hour in a sauce-pan, well covered,
with some good butter and a glassful of white wine;
when nearly done, add some flour, bouillon and
lemon-juice or mushrooms.

SOLES, in Holland style.

Scale the white side of the fish and skin the dark
one, cut off the fins and remove the gills and intestines, wash the fish, then soak in a little salt for
about an hour and wipe dry; roll in beaten egg and
crushed toast, and fry floating in hot lard; when
done, place on a colander and then on a hot plate,
garnish with a bunch of parsley dipped in hot lard,
and serve with fried potatoes (Pom. frids) and quartered lemons. To cook potatoes in this style, cut the
raw potatoes into slices, then into strips, dry them
with a cloth and fry floating in hot lard, stirring
them well; when they rise to the surface and turn
yellow, they are taken out with a strainer, placed on
a colander, and some fine salt sprinkled over them.

SPOONBILL OR PADDLEFISH.
(Treat like Sturgeon.)

STURGEON.

Take a medium-sized Shovel-nosed or a small Lake Sturgeon, wash, clean, and place it in the kettle; pour well-seasoned, cold bouillon over it, and boil until done. Spread a napkin over a long plate, lay the boiled fish on this, and serve with Holland sauce and melted butter. Sturgeon may also be baked.

TENCH, BLUE.

As soon as the fish are killed, clean but do not scale them, and pour boiling vinegar over them. In a stew-pot put water with salt, one onion, spice and a bayleaf, and boil; then add the fish, and boil until done. Serve with melted butter and potatoes.

TENCH, WITH DILL.

Clean, rub with salt and scale the Tench; then cut them into pieces. After having been well washed, they are boiled in salt-water and served with the following sauce: Set some milk on the fire, and when it boils, add a handful of coarsely chopped dill and a piece of butter; stir the yolks of three fresh eggs, a teaspoonful of salt, a tablespoonful of flour, in a little cold milk and mix this with the boiling milk; pour over the fish, add some grated nutmeg, then serve.

TENCH, in JELLY.*
(See Eel, in Jelly.)

STEWED TERRAPIN OR TURTLE.*

Put them into boiling water and boil rapidly or until the nails come off and the black skin loosens, which will be in about fifteen minutes; after this, put into fresh boiling water and boil until the lower shell cracks. This will require about half an hour or more. Now remove the lower shell, throw away the sand and gall bags, take the intestines out, and put the rest back into the same water, to boil for one hour more; now pick all the meat from the upper shell, cut the intestines into small pieces and add to the meat, pour over all some of the water in which it was cooked to make it saucy, and set aside until the next day. To finish, take a glassful of wine, one of cream, two tablespoonfuls of butter, the yellow of two hard-boiled eggs mashed very fine; salt and pepper to taste; this all you pour over the Terrapin-meat, put it on the fire and heat to boiling; then serve.

TURBOT AND HALIBUT.

Set this fish cold on the fire, and boil, or rather simmer, as directed in the General Recipés. The appearance of the fish may be improved by soaking it in milk before boiling. Serve with the same sauces as used for Salmon. See also Flounders.

TROUT, Blue.

The fish is killed and the blood saved in a little'
water; after cleaning, not scaling, the fish, cut a joint
out of the spinal column, and then lay the fish for a
little while in the water containing the blood; the
fish is then blued with boiling vinegar, exposing the
fish not longer than three minutes to the latter, however. In the kettle boil water with salt and whole
pepper; to this add the fish, let it boil for a second
or two, and then set aside to simmer for ten minutes.
Put on a plate, garnish with parsley and quartered
lemons, and serve with boiled potatoes and fresh
butter.

TROUT, Fried.

After cleaning and scaling the fish, scrape its skin
until it is rough to the touch; then open several eggs
into a dish and lay the trout for half an hour in it
(the eggs should cover the fish); then take it out and
roll in grated bread, covering the entire fish well, and
fry slowly with butter or bacon. Trout should be
killed as soon as out of the water, and should never
be washed afterward.

TROUT, with Aspic.

After the Trout has been boiled and cooled off
take it carefully out of the kettle, place it on a plate

and pour, repeatedly, half-stiffened meat jelly over it until the fish is well covered. Garnish with boiled eggs, Lobster-meat, parsley, and serve with vinegar and oil.

WHITEFISH.

Scale, clean and wash the fish, set on the fire with cold water and a little vinegar, spice, salt, onions and bayleaves. As soon as it boils move to the side of the range and simmer a little while. Serve with Holland sauce or browned butter and mustard. This most excellent noble lake fish may also be baked or fried.

INDEX.

CEREALINE FLAKES.

CINCINNATI, O., *December* 18, 1886.

I have, requested by Mr. Hugo Mulertt, prepared a meal of fried smoked fish (Lake Herrings) and Cerealine Flakes. I mixed two and one-half cupfuls of Cerealine Flakes with two cupfuls of cold water, set it aside to soak for a few minutes, then boiled the same for eight or ten minutes under frequent stirring, added one tablespoonful of good butter and seasoned with pepper, salt and nutmeg, and left it ten minutes longer on the stove. The fire should be moderate while boiling the Cerealine. I then fried the filet of two smoked fish in butter, and served them with the Cerealine. I declare it a delicious dish, well fitting together; and so do all who ate of it.

HERMAN G. UNSER,
Cook at the St. Nicholas Hotel,
Corner Fourth and Race Streets.

The CHRISTIAN MOERLEIN

BREWING COMPANY,

CINCINNATI, OHIO,

—Brewers and Bottlers of the Renowned—

"NATIONAL" EXPORT LAGER

A Genuine Old Lager Beer admirably suited for Table Use, and recommended by Physicians for the Weak and Convalescent.

FIRST PREMIUM,

Cin'ti Industrial Expositions 1881-82-83-84.

To meet the wants of our Retail Business, we have located permanently in our handsome quarters,

No. 132 WEST SIXTH STREET,

Third door west of Race, where can always be found a fresh Stock of *Oysters, Fish, Game and Poultry.* Suburban delivery. Telephone No. 846. Inspect our Retail Department. Yours respectfully,

J. E. FREY.

G. N. MERRYWEATHER,

CHOICE TEAS

—AND—

Fresh Roasted Coffees,

S. E. COR. SIXTH AND RACE STREETS,

CINCINNATI, O.

CORN STARCH

—FOR FOOD,—

As Manufactured by

THE A. ERKENBRECHER CO.

At CINCINNATI, OHIO,

I S THE QUEEN OF TABLE EDIBLES, and the most delicious of Maize preparations extant.

It is incomparably pure, healthful and economical, and a blessing alike to the sick and well, for children and adults.

It enters into the most recherche pastry, ices and dessert dishes, embracing Blanc-mange, Ice Cream, Puddings, Custards, Pies, etc., lending a peculiar delicacy and nutritious quality, and is, at once, a necessity and a luxury in every domestic storehouse. No edible Starch stands so high the world over.

SOLD BY GROCERS EVERYWHERE.

www.ingramcontent.com/pod-product-compliance
Lightning Source LLC
Chambersburg PA
CBHW022150090426
42742CB00010B/1450